Rosalee Glass

100 Years of Wisdom

To Guide You Thru Life's Ups and Downs

by

Rosalee Glass

YOUR TOTAL IMAGE PUBLISHING,
BEVERLY HILLS, CALIFORNIA

Published by   Your Total Image Publishers,
                      Beverly Hills, California

Library of Congress Catalog- In- Publication Data:

Glass, Rosalee.
Rosalee Glass 100 Years of Wisdom
To Guide You Thru Life's Ups and Downs

Rosalee Glass

ISBN: 978-1-929873-56-2

1.Self Help Techniques 2. Interpersonal Relationships 3. Psychology

Published in the United States of America

Dedication

To the apple of my eye, my daughter, Dr. Lillian Glass.
You are everything I ever dreamed you would become
and I am so incredibly proud of you. From the bottom
of my heart, I thank you for everything you have done
for me. God has truly blessed Me. It is an honor and a
privilege to have you as my precious daughter. You
are a miracle who has enriched my life beyond belief.
May God bless you always.

Acknowledgements

First and foremost, I wish to thank my beautiful and brilliant daughter who is the love of my life, Dr. Lillian Glass for making this book possible. I thank her for being the motivation, the strength and the backbone behind this project.

I also thank Your Total Image Publishing for publishing this book and their committed support for this project.

I thank my beloved late father Mendel Talerman, mother Perla, brother Jacob and sisters, Regina and Lola as well as my wonderful husband of 60 years Abraham Glass, and my beloved son, Manny Glass for their love and respect. May each of them rest in beautiful peace in heaven.

I thank Dr. Robert Huizinga for his encouragement and motivation in writing this book.

To Lisa Darrow for the cover shot and Magda Velasquez for several photographs in the book taken on behalf of Lifetouch Portrait Studios Inc. Target. I also thank Lillian Glass for the photos she took, which appear throughout the pages throughout this book.

Mr. Joe Solo at www.solostudios.net, I thank you for your cover design and for designing my website at www.rosaleeglass.com

And finally, I wish to also give thanks to all of the beautiful and tremendous people around the world whom I have met throughout my life, who have enriched and given such special meaning to my life.

Table of Contents

Forward by Dr. Lillian Glass

Since one is only as great as the shoulders on which they stand, I am proud to say that I stand on some pretty great shoulders - those of my mother, Rosalee Glass. She is my hero. I am sure that after you read this book, she will be your hero as well.

I have been blessed to have felt her love ever since babyhood, when she carried me in her arms, even when I may have been too big or heavy to carry. But she didn't mind. She was willing to sacrifice discomfort, just to make sure I was comforted - something she did through my entire life. This was and is her definition of genuine love for another person. It is *"when you think of the other person's comfort and happiness before your own."* The secure hugs and squeezes, warm, genuine smiles, and kind, loving, soothing words were the currency she used to assure me that I was loved throughout my life.

There are little moments when you are growing up that can mean the world to you. They help shape you into the person you are today. One such moment was on a rainy Miami day, when my mom decided to walk me to school before she went to work. As we walked together, we got caught in a heavy downpour. In order to not get my feet wet, she physically lifted me up above each and every puddle we came across. It was fun. We both laughed whenever she picked me up. When we finally arrived at my school, we were both drenched. So, my mom decided that we would both return home and play hooky (me from school and her from work). This turned out to be one of the best days of my life. Since we were already wet, we walked home and enjoyed the feel of warm rain dripping on both of our heads, faces, and skin. As soon as we came into the house, she dried me off and dressed me in warm dry clothes, as she did the same. She made me a sandwich and a warm cup of chicken noodle soup. Afterwards, we spent the rest of the day playing games, coloring, telling jokes, and laughing.

On one uniquely cold evening in Miami, with its' strong wind currents, I will never forget her opening up her cream colored wool coat and wrapping me in it as we both walked to and from the neighborhood market. I ended up walking backwards as I held on to her waist, snuggling under the inside of her coat, and feeling the warmth of her body heat. It made me feel safe- like I was back in her womb.

Decades later, whenever I recall these two experiences - her lifting me over the puddles on that rainy Miami day and her wrapping me inside of her coat on that cold Miami evening, it always brings a smile to my face and a warm cozy feeling bathes covers me from head to toe.

While she was the breadwinner of the family and worked long hours to make ends meet to put food on the family table, the time we both spent together was quality time. Then and now, I cherish the times we spent sunbathing on Miami Beach, taking nightly walks around the block, and smelling the fragrant flowers along the way. I have the best memories of our searching for the right outfits for me on our weekend clothes and shoe shopping expeditions.

As we chose my school and special occasion outfits, she instilled in me the art of matching, the use of contrast in selecting colors, and always looking for quality material and fine textures in clothing. She taught me the basics of dressing and grooming and always smelling good and its' importance in terms of how others perceive you in the world.

In grade school, whenever I encountered nasty Toxic mean girls, with their stupid cliques, secret telling, and cruel teasing, my mom was always there to comfort me. She wiped away my tears, hugged me tightly, pulled me close to her chest, soothed me, and calmed me down by sharing one of her reassuring sayings - her words of wisdom. They always seemed to comfort me.

As a 13 - year old, I went to my first grown up party at a fancy Miami Beach hotel with a friend. My friend's parents were celebrating their wedding anniversary. As soon as we arrived, my friend went off with her cousins and left me all alone at the table, with no one to talk to and nothing to do. So, I made a phone call to my mom from the party to tell her how awful and out of place, I felt. I asked her and my dad to come pick me up and take me home. But instead of rushing to get me, my mom told me to pretend I was a journalist. She suggested I go up to as many people as possible, introduce myself, and ask them questions about themselves. She said that after I did this, I should call her back and let her know if I still needed to be picked up and taken home.

I forgot to call her back because I ended up having one the best times in my life. I met so many people - all adults who did so many interesting things. I met a herpetologist (a snake expert), a college professor, and several attorneys. I quickly discovered that people loved talking about themselves and I loved listening to them. It was my mom's brilliant suggestion that changed my life forever. It set me on the right path in life. It cured me of my shyness and showed me that I could talk to anyone, from any walk of life. Her sound advice was something that has stood me well throughout my life. It even got me to become a journalist, among the other things which I have done in my career.

It is my mother's words of wisdom that has allowed me to achieve heights in my life from getting my PhD at the young age of 24, to writing over 20 books, to being a television commentator, lecturer, body language expert, traveling the world as a lecturer, being a mediator, jury and litigation consultant, to having the opportunity to serve as an expert witness in human behavior in both criminal and civil cases.

As you read the first section of the book about my mother's life, you will laugh and perhaps even shed a tear or two.

In the second half of the book, as you read her original words of wisdom and look at the photos taken of her throughout her life's adventures, it may inspire, encourage, and motivate you. You will learn as much as I have learned from this brilliant woman. Her words will continue to resonate with you, as they do with me on a daily basis.

While I have earned the privilege of being called "Dr. Glass," as a result of my formal education, I consider my mom, Rosalee Glass, to be the real "Dr. Glass." After reading and applying her 100 years of knowledge and wisdom as reflected by her original words of wisdom she is sharing with you throughout this book, I am sure you will agree with me.

Just as her words of wisdom have motivated and empowered me through the ups and downs of my life, I am certain they will do the same for you.
Lillian Glass PhD

Rosalee holding baby Lily at 9 months and at 18 months

Rosalee still holding Lillian

Part I –A Life of Ups and Downs and Twists and Turns

Chapter 1 A Bright Happy Rosalee Is Born

I was born on a cold winter's day in 1917 on the 28th of January in Warsaw, Poland at Baby Jesus Hospital, (Dzjachontka Jesus). As soon as my mother, Perla gave birth to me, she said her first words were *"A Rayzele has been born."* She named me after her maternal grandmother. She told anyone who would listen that as soon as I came out of the womb, I had a smile on my face.

I was born in Baby Jesus Hospital, (Dzjachontka Jesus) in Warsaw, Poland on January 28,1917.

I was a very happy, bright, energetic child. I loved my family, especially my father, Mendel Talerman, a shoe salesman and manufacturer. He and I had a special bond. I was the "apple of his eye." He loved to hear me sing all the songs I learned from the nuns at the Catholic school I attended near my home. He especially loved the song I sang in Polish about a train. It has been over 96 years and I still remember the words to the song and I can sing it.

"It doesn't matter what you sing or how you sound when you sing. Just sing from your heart because singing is healing." My father also liked to sing to me. In fact, he always used to sing a special song in Yiddish to me. The song

had my name in it - *"Rayzele."* It was my favorite song and I felt so happy whenever I heard him singing it to me.

He was a very intelligent man. He always had wise sayings, which he always shared with me and my sisters and brother. They seemed to open up my developing mind. He had a special saying ready for any life situation which arose. I usually found comfort in his words of wisdom. I particularly remember one quote from him - *"the world is made up of a lot of different worlds."* To me, that saying meant that there was a big world out there with many people living their lives in their own little worlds.

A good little girl, I loved to help my father with all aspects of his shoe business. From seeing how hard he worked, I learned early on, how dedication, integrity, and perseverance was essential to achieve any goal.

Mendel Talerman, my wonderful father.

Chapter 2 - Teen Entrepreneur

"If you believe you can do something, don't let anyone ever tell you that you can't."

My parents and extended family seemed to be impressed at how determined I was as a little girl. I once overheard my mother bragging about me to a neighbor. She said that of all her children, she was never worried about me. I would be a success in life because I accomplished whatever I set my mind to do. She was most likely was referring to the time I taught myself to sew when I was 10. I simply wouldn't give up until I mastered it.

Me at 10 years old (2ⁿᵈ to l) with sister Regina (l), brother Jacob, and sister Lola.(r)

I made a shirt for my little sister Lola, my little brother Jacob, older sister Regina, and one for my father. Looking back, they may not have been the greatest looking shirts, but my father said they were beautiful. That encouraged me to make more shirts. The more shirts I made, the better I got at making them.

At 14, I became so adept at sewing, I began making tailored men's shirts. Many of our neighbors admired the workmanship of my shirts and began buying them for themselves and for their family members. That was when I became a bona fide businesswoman - making men' shirts on demand for people in the neighborhood.

A year later, at 15, without anyone's prompting, I decided to try my luck and visited a local men's store near my home to see if the store owner wanted to purchase some of my hand made shirts to sell to his customers. As soon as the owner saw my shirts and examined their quality, he jumped at the chance to sell them. He not only paid me handsomely for each shirt, he offered me a large retainer fee salary to make shirts on demand for all of his customers.

I seemed to have an entrepreneurial spirit. I wanted to grow my business even bigger. I decided that my shirts should be available to even more men who shopped at different stores. But there were naysayers – those who tried to discourage me. My own mother was one of these naysayers.

If you think you can do something, don't let anyone tell you different."

She thought I was doing just fine with my small business, making shirts on demand and receiving a steady stipend from the local men's shop. But I wanted to go bigger. I wanted to sell my shirts to not just one store, but many stores. I was not content with the status quo. I had bigger ideas. But my mother worried that I might fail at my goal. She asked me what I would do if I expanded my business and it failed. I told her that I would try again until I succeeded. Unlike my mother, my father encouraged me to take a risk and go for it. So that is exactly what I did.

Being a self-motivated teenager, with no financial backing from anyone, I ended up creating my own successful shirt making factory at 18. I employed 10 women. They allowed me to sell my shirts to numerous exclusive men's clothing stores throughout Warsaw.

In order to keep up with the high customer demand, I invested the money I earned from selling the shirts, and bought several Singer sewing machines. I lined them up side by side in the back room of my parent's home. This allowed the women I employed to sew even more shirts I designed.

"Always try! It may work out in your favor."

Me at 18 years old when I began my own men's shirt making business, with 10 employe

Chapter 3 - Finding True Love

"If you have love in your heart, you will be loved"

Also when I was 18, an extremely handsome and talented young violin player, 10 years older than me, who lived nearby, apparently had a crush on me.

One day, he decided to serenade me with his violin playing, right outside my window in front of my home with the same song my father used to sing to me - *"Rayzele."* When I looked out the window to see who was playing this beautiful music, I saw a man who was so handsome. He looked like a movie star.

Abraham Glass, the love of my life who serenaded me with his violin.

My mother, also liked what she heard and saw. So, she invited this violin player to come into our home. Very protective over me, she asked him all about him until she felt comfortable to formally introduce to me. As soon as I looked into his eyes, I had himself butterflies in my stomach.

Me with my mother, Perla standing behind me.

Besides his impressive musical talent, I found him to be so smart, lively, and charismatic after we spoke and got to know one another. Seeing how we couldn't stop talking with one another, my mother invited him to stay for dinner.

Now the entire family met him and they too seemed to fall in love with him, especially after he gave us a violin concert after dinner.

Abraham Glass became a constant presence in our home, coming over for meals, as he courted me. My mother thought he would be a wonderful match for me and encouraged us to become a couple.

A year later, Abraham asked my father for permission to marry me. My father said to him *"You are too old for her. You are ten years older."* Abraham's reply was *"Even though your daughter is 19, she is very mature and needs a mature man."* Apparently, that was a good enough response for my father. He finally gave Abraham permission to marry me.

Our wedding was beautiful. I not only made my own wedding dress, I made dresses for my mother and sister and shirts for my father, brother, and new husband.

Shortly after our wedding and hopes for a beautiful life together, life took an unexpected turn that was anything but beautiful.

Chapter 4 - Nazi Message of Hate

"When you pay careful attention to what's going on around you, will you clearly see the message the universe is giving you about what direction to take in life."

One afternoon, while my husband and I went out for a stroll, we encountered a group of men dressed in Nazi uniforms. They were lined up next to one another, each one having their arm on the shoulder of the soldier in front of them. One of the soldiers broke away from the line, came up to me, and slapped me very hard across my face. I was shocked and almost fell backwards. I said nothing. Then he looked directly at me and said *"You should thank me for this!"*

The Nazi was eagerly waiting for Abraham to react and fight back. But Abraham was way too clever. He knew exactly what would happen if he fought back to defend my honor. In no uncertain terms, he would have been shot to death. So, he did all that he could to hold back his anger. As a result of his controlled restraint, the group of Nazi's let him and me leave without further incident.

Chapter 5- On the Run

"Always listen to your heart and your instincts! Act upon them! If they tell you something is wrong – it is!

Immediately after this shocking incident, Abraham and I made the decision to leave Warsaw as soon as possible. It was decided that Abraham would go to northern Poland first. Our plan was for him to search for lodging and then send word via messenger as to his exact location. Then, I would join him. In the meantime, I moved back into my parent's home.

"When you are well dressed and well - groomed people will treat you with respect."

Dressed in his finest tailored coat and wearing elegant leather gloves, Abraham was well- dressed and well-groomed. He did not look disheveled, like the other people who were also attempting to cross the border. As he approached the border, he observed that it was not so easy to cross. Countless people were not only being turned away, they were being beaten by Nazi soldiers.

Replica of the Nazi hat Abraham found on the ground, put on his head, and crossed the border.

Shortly before Abraham approached the border, fate was definitely with him. Being on high alert and carefully observing everything around him, he happened to look down at the ground and noticed a Nazi hat, which some Nazi must have inadvertently dropped. Abraham immediately picked up the hat, complete with Nazi insignias on it, and boldly placed it on his head.

Nazi soldiers making the "Heil Hitler" salute at a border crossing, similar to the salute they gave Abraham.

Then Abraham calmly and confidently walked to the border gate. As he was walking through the border, he suddenly noticed that the soldiers standing guard, immediately stood at attention, clicked their heels, and saluted to him with their outstretched arms making the Nazi salute. They verbally greeted him with a loud *"Heil Hitler."* Abraham gave them a nod and a smile as he calmly walked across the border.

Apparently, the hat on Abraham's head was that of a high ranking Nazi officer. That hat, combined with his elegant clothing (a long, custom made, well-tailored coat) new shiny shoes, and impeccable posture, (with his shoulders back and his head held high), allowed the border guards to believe that the man walking across the border was a bona fide Nazi officer. They never imagined he was a despised Jew trying to save his life, so that he could subsequently save his family. The smile he had on his face as he crossed the border reflected his delight at being able to successfully fool the Nazi guards into thinking he was one of their own.

As Abraham was now safely across the border, he found a horse and buggy driver to take him to northern Poland. He successfully made it to Bialystok, Poland.

There, he found a family living in a farm house. He paid them for a room in their home and even gave them extra money to cover costs whenever I and my family would arrive. Now that he was settled in Bialystok, he sent a letter to my parent's home in Warsaw via messenger. I received it a few days later.

The letter contained the exact location of the farmhouse and it said to make sure I bring my entire family because there was there was plenty of room. It also said to load up our knapsacks with anything we could barter for food. And finally it said to make sure to bring plenty of bread and goose fat.

I immediately began packing and assumed my family would do the same and would come with me. But they refused to come. They said things would get better and had to stay because of all their belongings, their furniture, and their home. Even though I pleaded with them, it fell on deaf ears. With the exception of my brother, they all insisted on staying.

Being so closely connected to my father, I saw through his eyes that he wanted to come with me. I asked him again. He told me that my mother wouldn't leave and in good conscience, he couldn't leave his wife behind. So against his better judgement, he decided to stay with her. I knew this would be the last time I would ever see my father. Right before I was getting ready to leave, he placed both his hands on my head and recited a Hebrew blessing over me. He kissed my head. I saw tears rolling down his cheeks.

My mother on the other hand, was solemn and silent. She couldn't seem to bring herself to say goodbye, kiss, or even hug me. Perhaps she knew deep down, that would never see me again and the parting may have been too painful for her to bear. So, she shut down emotionally, as a way of coping with her losing me. But as a gesture of motherly love and concern, just before I left the house, she put her favorite emerald green shawl around my head and shoulders so I would be warm on my journey.

My younger brother Jacob and I left carrying heavy knapsacks on our backs. We set forth on foot towards the border. As we walked quite a while, I began to observe that things had gone from bad to worse since that shocking slap I received across my face by that

Nazi soldier. Suddenly that slap seemed like a minor incident compared to what I was now seeing the Nazi's do right in front of my eyes.

It shocked me to see Nazi's grab crying babies from their mother's arms and throw their screaming babies out of windows in broad daylight. I saw so many women and men getting kicked repeatedly and endure severe bloody beatings with Nazi soldier's sticks and rifles. I saw people being shot in the back and falling to the ground as a lifeless corpse. I saw countless dead bodies - bodies of innocent men, women, and children. It sickened me that I had to step over so many dead bodies lying in the street. I even saw a horse being shot. People later started to cut it up in order to eat the meat. I couldn't believe what my eyes were seeing. It was horrible. It was like having the worst nightmare.

As I numbly continued to walk, I heard a loud blood curdling scream. There was a woman lying under a tree. As I ran over to her, I quickly discovered her screams were due to her pain of just giving birth to a baby. I immediately pulled off the emerald green shawl my mother gave me and I wrapped the naked infant in it so that it would be warm and have protection from the elements.

Photo of a Nazi soldier at the border occupied by Germans in Warsaw, Poland.

"Calm down and think what to do next."

"Luck is doing the right thing and taking a chance."

Finally, my brother and I reached the boarder. There were two lines - one for Jews and one for Gentiles. As soon as I saw Jews getting slapped and beaten in the line marked for Jews, I thought, *"there is no way I'm going to go into that line."* So, my brother and I went to the line marked for Gentiles. I kept my cool and remained focused. My only thought was to get across the border. As I waited in line, I removed my heavy knapsack and pushed it along the line with my feet.

Finally, it was my turn to be checked by the Nazi soldier standing on front of me. But before he had a chance to speak, putting on a German accent, I boldly asked him if he could please help me lift the knapsack on to my back. This over 6 foot Nazi, tried to pick up my heavy knapsack to place on my back, but he could hardly lift it. He immediately burst out laughing at the absurdity of how he was twice my size and couldn't lift it, but a little 5-foot girl, half his size could carry that same heavy knapsack on her back. Finally, after lifting it on to my back as he continued to laugh, I politely thanked him, using my best German accent and with my brother following right behind me, we took off running as fast as we could.

"Never Look Back. Always Go Forward"

I didn't even feel the weight of the heavy knapsack on my back as the adrenalin rushed through my body. I didn't even feel the huge water blister that formed on my forehead, along with my scraped knees, after tipping over a rock and falling flat on my face while running so fast. My only concern was that I didn't injure the baby I was now carrying in my belly. I was pregnant.

Relieved I made it safely across to the other side of the German border, I was now in Russian territory. I didn't know it at the time. I felt relieved that I was now safe. Standing nearby, was a man with a horse and buggy. I offered him money to take me and my brother to the location where my husband had written in his letter for me to come and meet him. We traveled 122 miles from Warsaw to Bialystok, in northern Poland.

As soon as I arrived at the designated location, my husband saw me from a distance. Immediately, he ran to the horse and buggy and we tightly embraced one another. We were both thrilled to see one another after being apart for what seemed like an eternity.

As soon as I entered the house my husband secured for us, I placed the goose fat, bread, and a bar of soap on the table for the family in who's house we would be living. They were very appreciative of the gesture.

Months later, in that home, I gave birth to a baby boy, we named Elias. I was elated with my new son. I so happy that he, my husband, brother and I were all safe from the Nazi's. Now I had hope that my life would turn around for the better. But instead, it took a turn for the worse.

Chapter 6 - Unwillingly Taken to Siberia

One May night, around midnight, a uniformed soldier vigorously knocked on the door of our home and began shouting in some strange language. I couldn't understand what he was saying. I quickly figured out that the soldier was Russian.

Even though I didn't know the exact words he was saying, he made himself perfectly clear as he loudly demanded and gestured that my husband and I, along with my brother immediately gather our things and the and follow him. I held my baby securely against my chest as he roughly shouted for us to get into the open truck, situated in front of him.

Not having any idea where I was headed, I continued to hold my baby tightly, as we were then forced from that open truck into a people-packed cattle car, with no toilet facilities, food, or water.

It was scary to be in that cattle car and not knowing where we were going. There was no light. It was so dark and frightening. All we heard was the sound of the train as we felt its' rocking movement along the train tracks.

Cattle cars were used to transport political prisoners from Poland to Siberia.

After what seemed like weeks, we were transported to a remote area in Archangelsk, north of Siberia in Russia. The area was called Glubakowski Leso Punkt. Little did I know that we were taken there to this prison camp and officially declared "prisoners of war." We were taken there to do slave labor.

Living conditions in the tiny room in the prison camp were extremely harsh. We had a little water and only a small slice of daily bread, that I received only after having to stand in a long line. There was also the occasional potato which I had to grow in order to eat. Once in a while, every few weeks, it was announced over a radio speaker in the middle of the night, that cow parts were available. So, I had to walk miles and miles in the freezing snow, across the horizon, in order to stand in line for hours, just to get a small piece of raw meat. I often bared the bitter cold and waited in line a second time, just so I could get more meat for my starving family. The cold was unbearable. I had no warm clothes, only a thin dress and a thin jacket. My legs froze. I got frostbite. It was painful.

Without food and proper nutrients, I was no longer able to produce breast milk for my baby. As Elias continually cried from hunger, I continually tried to feed him. But no breast milk came out. Bread and water was not enough for an infant. I felt terribly helpless. As a result, my baby Elias tragically starved to death. He died in my arms. I was absolutely devastated. This poor baby had nothing to eat and was freezing to death and there was absolutely nothing I could do for him. I would often awake from my sleep in terror, realizing that my baby was no longer alive.

Not prepared for the freezing temperatures of the Siberian winters, in the Siberian forest, I continued to suffer greatly from the pain of the bitter cold on the dark days and long nights. I only had the thin clothing on my back that I came with when the Russian soldier initially came to the door in the middle of the night, insisting we all into the cattle car.

As a forced laborer, we were constantly under the watchful eyes of prison guards who waked back and forth, making sure we did what we were told. If anyone got out of line and didn't do what they said, they were immediately shot. So I was in constant fear of being shot. The soldiers made me break up ice on the ground with a with an iron pole. Abraham's forced labor was not much better. His job was to locate the roots of trees so that everyone would know where to plant the potatoes which we grew for food.

"Bad times are not forever"

On a daily basis, I witnessed so many people dying in the Siberian prison camp. Almost everyone there had such a bleak view of what their future held. But I absolutely refused to give in to negative thoughts. I strongly believed that this situation would not be forever and that this harsh life would eventually turn around for the better. I said this to myself and to my husband over and over, several times a day. I believed it wholeheartedly. I even tried to motivate many of prisoners around me who had tragically given up hope and who no longer wanted to live.

"Even in the coldest and saddest days, the SUN can still come out to SHINE for YOU."

Since I was the only one keeping a positive attitude many prisoners seemed to be drawn to me and to what I had to say. They would seek me out and ask me to say something positive to them- a word- a phrase just to make them feel a little better. They called me their *"ray of sunshine."* I will never forget one prisoner grabbing my hands and crying. He said all he thought bout was dying, but I inspired him to never give up. This moved me.

Even though I suffered terribly and was emotionally distraught after losing my precious baby boy, I managed to get outside of my own pain. I managed to be of help to others around me and motivate them. That was what was helping me to heal emotionally.

Chapter 7 -Further Loss Along Parts Unknown

Unbeknownst to me the war had finally ended. One day I, along with all of the other "prisoners of war," including my brother Jacob, were gathered, forced into a train and taken to yet another remote destination - Kazakhstan, located over 1500 miles away from Siberia. But at the time, I had no idea where the train was headed. All I knew was that the train ride was very long and the cattle car was closed and dark. I didn't know whether it was day or night. It seemed to be a repeat of our travel experience from Bialystok, Poland to Siberia. It was equally as frightening. Once again there was no food, water, or bathroom facilities.

Train tracks like the ones in Russia on which the cattle car transported me and my family when we were unknowingly taken to Kazakhstan.

Suddenly, on the way to my unknown destination, which we later discovered to be Kazakhstan, the train suddenly stopped in a place called Saratov, Russia. There, a group of uniformed female nurses boarded the train. The nurses asked if anyone needed medical attention. Because it was such an unusual occurrence and because we didn't know who these people were or who they represented, no one dared to volunteer that they had a problem. The reality is that everyone had a problem. The living conditions were so poor and the prison camp, that everyone need treatment for one thing or another. Nevertheless, we all kept quiet. Suddenly, one of the former prisoners of war in the cattle car opened his big mouth and pointed to my brother, Jacob. He told the nurses something about Jacob that was not his concern. He reported that Jacob had an infected foot.

As a result, Jacob was removed from the train. Both my husband and I pleaded with the nurses to not take Jacob. We said we would take care of his foot. But they ignored us and carried Jacob off the train. At first I was inconsolable. I couldn't bear to lose yet another family member.

But then, I calmed myself down with the thought that perhaps Jacob's foot would be treated and afterwards, the nurses would put him on another train whereby he would be taken to the same destination where I was headed. I sincerely believed that Jacob would ultimately be joining me and Abraham. Unfortunately, that was be the case.

My beloved brother Jacob Talerman pulled off a train, forced into the Russian Army and never heard from again.

Those nurses took Jacob Talerman to a hospital in Saratov, where they treated his foot injury. But instead of putting him on a train to join me and my husband in Kazakhstan, like I assumed, Jacob never came. His name was changed to a Russian name. He was now Jakobavich Mendelevich (son of Mendel). He was forcibly drafted into the Russian Army. Much to my despair, there was no record of whatever happened to him after he was taken into the Russian army.

It was only through the efforts of the Red Cross, decades later, that I found out Jacob was taken into the Russian army against his will. There is no further record of him or his whereabouts.

Living In A Chicken Coup In Kazakhstan

With no money, food, or a place to live, Abraham and I were deposited by the Russians from the train into an area we found so muddy, our shoes remained in the thick mud whenever we wanted to take a step forward.

Chicken coup, similar to the one in which my husband and I lived in Kazakhstan.

Ultimately, my husband and I found shelter in a chicken coop. We made it our home and we lived together with the chickens. We were on one side of the coup and the chickens were on the other side.

> *"You can learn a lot from anyone - even animals."*

I really liked those chickens. I learned a lot about their behaviors. I discovered they were very intelligent animals and each had unique personalities. Perhaps that is why I hate eating chicken to this day.

While in Kazakhstan, Abraham began making leather shoes and selling shoes on the black market. This allowed us to eat more nourishing food, which was also purchased on the black market. It was the only option where to shop. But all too often, the food was not fresh and it made us sick.

In Kazakhstan, we decided to have another child. I naturally delivered a beautiful, blond baby girl named Perlie. Tragically, because of the poor living conditions, poor nutrition, and no medical care, she died as a toddler. She succumbed to the harsh environment and to tuberculosis. Having lost one child to the brutal conditions of war, here I was having to bury yet another baby. I was completely devastated. I couldn't eat or sleep. I could hardly function.

Chapter 8 - German Displaced Persons (DP) Camp

Shortly after my daughter Perlie's death, still in severe mourning, my husband and I were rounded up once again and taken by train to a Displaced Person's Camp in Feldafing, Germany.

While conditions were better than living in a chicken coup, they were still depressing. While food was more available, I still had to endure long lines to get food for myself and now for my new child, a baby boy I named after my father Mendel, whom I called Manny. Manny was a delight. As a baby, he was exceptionally bright. He walked and talked earlier than most babies.

Displaced Person's Camp where I lived in Feldafing, Germany

In order to secure money for enough food and proper medical care, I once again called upon my sewing skills. While in the DP camp, I noticed that many of the women lacked bras. So I used my own bra as a pattern and sewed hand-made bras for women to purchase. As a result, I was able to earn a living. This helped care for the needs of my small family.

One day, baby Manny ran outside and I could not find him. Frantic, I looked everywhere. I finally found him at the camp's school. Even though he was too young, he wanted to go to school and be with the other boys. So at a very early age, Manny attended school.

The school took a photo of all the students at the in the Feldefing DP camp. Little Manny is also in that photo. You can see his little head sticking out in the second row, forth from the left, wearing a little cap, as he is the youngest child in attendance.

Baby Manny 2nd row 4th from the left with his little head sticking out for a school photo in Feldefing, Germany DP Camp.

While in the DP Camp, Abraham became very ill with lung problems. He got so sick that he was forced to leave the camp and enter a hospital, located a very far distance away from the camp. I was so worried about Abraham. I didn't know if he would live or die.

Because of the distance, I couldn't visit Abraham every day. I had to stay at the camp to care for Manny and sew the bras in order to earn money so that I could afford the periodic train rides to visit Abraham.

During his lengthy hospital stay, Abraham ended up having an operation where one of his infected lungs was removed. Although it deformed his chest, leaving a large indentation it it, the operation was a success in that it helped him to survive.

Shortly after he returned to the DP camp from being in the hospital for so long, we applied to come to the

United States. Luckily, and our application was granted.

Chapter 9- God Bless America

In order to get the United States, Manny, Abraham and I had to endure an intestinally tortured two- week ship ride. We experienced constant nausea due to seasickness as we traversed across the choppy Atlantic Ocean aboard the "General Muir," in route to New Orleans, Louisiana. I didn't mind it because I knew that it was only temporary. I knew I would soon be in the land of the free- America.

The General Muir, which transported me and my family to the USA.

The second I landed on American soil at the port of entry in New Orleans, I cried. Tears rolled down my cheeks as I bent down, kissed the ground, and spoke the words, *"God Bless America."* Whenever I sing tor I hear the song "God Bless America," I am moved. I know the true meaning of what those words meant for me.

I was so grateful to finally be in the land where there was freedom from oppression. I was now in place where I could have renewed hope for a new life with my loving husband and precious son.

Almost immediately after I set foot in New Orleans, the three of us were given one- way train tickets to Miami, Florida, courtesy of the American Jewish Federation, an organization to which I will always be grateful.

How Miami looked in 1951 when I first arrive there.

Upon arriving in Miami, which was clean, pristine, bright, and sunny, my first thought was, *"I landed in heaven."* For the first time in years, I was able to smile again. But my smile didn't last long when I received formal word that my beloved father, mother, and two sisters had all perished in the Holocaust, thereby making me the sole survivor. The reality of dealing with this was news a shock.

Even through all my grieving, I was still able to feel that there was hope. I decided that the most important thing I could do, now that I was in my new country, was to get pregnant and have a baby. This baby would become my "American Dream." This baby would help me heal from the agony of my past and from all the tragedy and loss I encountered. I felt that having this baby would give me a renewed reason to live. In my mind, I envisioned how I and my baby to be, would both learn and grow together in this new country.

Luck was on my side as my wish came true. I became pregnant a year after arriving in the USA. During my pregnancy, Abraham and I didn't attend birthing classes. Instead, we regularly attended English classes, where we learned to speak our new language and adapt to our new culture. While we were learning English, so was my son Manny. He was learning it in grade school. Soon Manny had a sister. I gave birth to a girl I wanted so much.

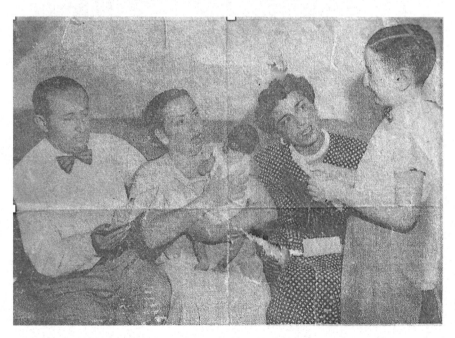

Abraham, me, Baby Lily, the journalist who did the interview Connie Gee, and Manny who read his poem for an article which appeared in the Miami Daily News.

I named my beautiful, healthy, 8 pound 2 oz. baby, born at 8:31AM in Miami Beach, Florida, Lily. But the nurse in the hospital said *"No her name is Lillian. Lily is her nickname."* Instead of arguing with the nurse, I let her write Lillian on the birth certificate. Actually I liked the Ann at the end of the name Lily. It was as though I was not only giving my baby the name I chose for her (Lily) now, she had additional name (Ann). So my baby was called Lillian.

A newspaper in Miami, the *Miami Daily News*, did a feature story about new immigrants and interviewed me. I liked how they accurately described Abraham and I as being a *"radiantly happy couple."* We were radiantly happy to be in the USA. In the article, Abraham was quoted as saying *"I like the people here with all my heart because I can live free in this country."* Even young Manny's poem which he wrote was quoted in the paper as it said *" I like the morning. I like the night. I like America with my life."*

Chapter 10 - Brand New Life in Miami

Shortly after learning English, Abraham was given vocational training as a watchmaker. He worked in the trade for a little while, until he discovered he had tuberculosis. He immediately had to go to a sanatorium at the Jewish Hospital in Denver, Colorado, which specialized in treating respiratory diseases. He stayed there over two and a half years, leaving me alone to care for my two children.

I had with no income, except for the $1 a day I received for food and the 50 cents a day I received to feed each child This was graciously provided by the Jewish Federation. Gratefully, they also paid for my rent. Because of them, I was able to have a safe place to live. When Abraham finally returned from Denver, he found work in his new trade as a watchmaker, which brought us more income. Now, we no longer had to rely on the goodness of the Jewish Federation for financial help.

Abraham always knew he had a lazy eye. But now, as a watchmaker, where he added additional eye strain, he noticed that it became harder to focus out of that eye. One day, he discovered he could no longer see out of it. Now completely blind in that eye, it became impossible for him to continue his work as a watchmaker, where vision was essential.

Now I had to become the breadwinner to support my family. Once again, I called upon my sewing skills and got a job making draperies. Abraham was now the house husband, way before it was popular.

He took the children to school, shopping, to doctor and dental appointments, attended PTA meetings, cleaned the house, and prepared meals.

Me (r) and Lillian (l)posing in bathing suits in Miami Beach as Manny, in the far right corner reads a book .

While this arrangement worked, I couldn't stand that I worked such long hours, didn't make much money, and didn't get to spend enough time with my precious children. I didn't like that I could only spent time with them at the beach on the weekends. Too often, I arrived home late at night when they were asleep. I briefly saw them in the morning before I had to take a series of buses to work.

"When you're independent, you can play your own drum any way you like."

So I decided to open my own drapery manufacturing shop, where I would no longer be at the mercy of others. I would be my own boss. I would do the creative work, while Abraham would do the business.

Now, I was not only able to see my children, on weekends, I could spend more time with them before they went to school and when they came directly to my drapery shop right after school.

Working together in business with Abraham and keeping my children close was a dream come true. Working for myself, allowed me to make more money and helped put both children through college. This was my only goal. It was my "American dream" come true.

Chapter 11-California Here I Come!

Shortly after I retired from my drapery business and closed up shop, Abraham and I moved west to California, in order to be closer to our daughter, Lillian. We moved to a luxurious retirement community in Laguna Hills, California, where we became involved in numerous activities and made many new friends. Since Abraham loved to cook, he invited new friends over for his special meals, while I served as the hostess. For next 15 years, our life together was the most stress free it had ever been.

"Losing someone you love is the worst pain possible. Knowing that you treated them well throughout their life and gave them lots of love helps ease your pain."

But then, Abraham passed away at the age of 90. It was hard for me to adjust to a life without Abraham, especially after being at one another's side for 60 years. But somehow, I managed. I made new friends and began new activities. I knew this is what Abraham would have wanted for me.

My beloved husband of 60 years, Abraham Glass.

Although I was deeply saddened by Abraham's death, I found comfort knowing that our marriage was based on true mutual love. I always felt respected, loved, and adored by him since day one. While he treated me like a Queen, I treated him like a King in return. That is why our marriage worked so well for 60 years.

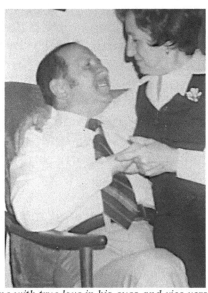

Abraham looking at me with true love in his eyes and vice versa.

Three years after Abraham died, my life took a devastating twist.

My brilliant, and wonderful son, Manny, with his electric personality and a tremendous sense of humor, whom I absolutely adored, who was the same son who as a little boy, came to America with me from Germany, aboard the "General Muir," had been tragically killed by an incompetent physician.

Manny wanted was getting his PhD. He wanted to change careers and open a nutrition clinic in Florida. But first, he wanted to observe how others did it. So he went to Hunterdon, New Jersey and stayed doctor's nutrition and wellness center. Manny had asthma and the doctor who owned the nutrition clinic took Manny off of all of his medications at once instead of taking him off the medications slowly. As a result, Manny went into anaphylactic shock. He was immediately taken to the local hospital.

While in the hospital emergency room, a young inexperienced doctor, who was only a doctor for seven months, intubated Manny improperly by putting a tube down the wrong pathway of his throat. As a result, Manny became a vegetable and died.

To make matters worse, this same doctor who killed Manny was so cold, insensitive, and unfeeling. His lack of compassion and sympathy only deepened my pain.

To say this emotionally eviscerated me as well as Lillian, would be an understatement. I had already lost two children during the war's deplorable conditions. Now I lost my one in a million son to the hands of an incompetent and ice-cold uncaring doctor.

Even though there was a malpractice suit against the doctor and the hospital, which was settled out of court, no amount of restitution could ever ease the pain of this horrific tragedy and this devastating and senseless loss. I would give back every penny just to see Manny smile and hear one of his jokes again.

The only thing for which I was grateful was that his father, who adored him, died three years earlier and didn't have to witness and suffer the agony of his beloved son and best friend's death.

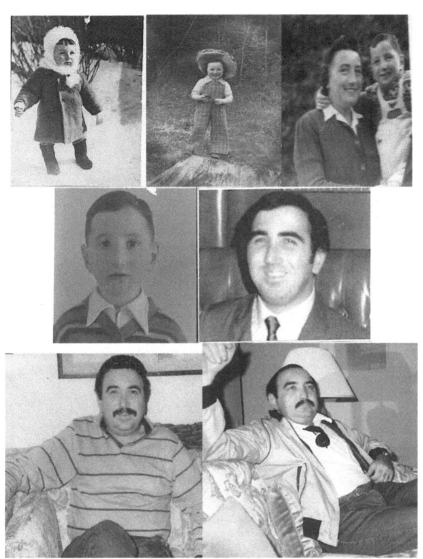

My brilliant and wonderful late son, Manny Glass at various stages of his life.

Manny Mendell Glass

February 5, 1945 to February 5, 1999

Manny was an inspiration to us all.
His warmth, effervescence,
good nature, great sense of humor,
sweet disposition, brilliant mind,
and uncanny insight into people
will always be remembered.
He touched so many while living
out his life's mission
"to help his fellow man."

May God bless him and
may he always be remembered with love.

Manny and Abraham Glass side by side in death at Hillside Memorial Park in Los Angeles.

Chapter 12- Manhattan Life, Jet Setting, and a Whole New Career
"Think about what to do next."

With Abraham and Manny gone, my daughter Lillian, didn't want me to be alone. So, she moved me into her beautiful New York City apartment.

It didn't matter where I lived or how beautiful a place it was, I was despondent. In fact, I didn't feel like living any longer. But somehow, I managed to regain my inner strength and *"think about what to do next."*

My recent tragic losses convinced me that now I had to embrace my life and live it to the fullest. I needed to take advantage of all it had to offer. That is when I decided to do things I never did before from taking Tai Chi, Tango dancing, French classes, to piano lessons.

While living in NYC, I often accompanied Lillian to the television shows on which she appeared as an expert. I was also her guest at many black tie charity events she attended. I loved going to them and getting dressed up in style. For the first time my life, I ate at the finest restaurants, went to museums, galleries, and to theatre openings. It was a whole new world for me. I also accompanied Lillian to the various lectures she gave around the country and around the world.

In traveling with her, whenever I passed through the security checkpoints at various airports across the country, it was not uncommon for a fellow passenger or a TSA employee to tell me they had seen me on TV or even to ask me for an autograph.

The more I traveled with Lillian, throughout the years, the more I experienced people asking me if I was an actress. Some people said they thought I resembled the actress in *Golden Girls*, Betty White, but neither I nor Lillian ever saw the resemblance, with the exception that both Betty and I are both petite, blond, and had a similar hairdo.

When I later moved back to LA with Lillian, I discovered why she and I really had the same hairdo. We shared the same hairdresser in Beverly Hills.

But Betty White, herself saw the resemblance between us. One day, by chance, we both met one another at our mutual hairdresser's salon. Betty remarked that we could be sisters. In jest, she even began introducing me to our mutual hairdresser as her "*long lost sister.*"

Because of all of the attention I kept getting about my looking like an actress, I thought it would be fun to enroll in an acting class in NYC. It turned out really liked acting. Soon, I got several talent agents, who sent me on many auditions. I even appeared in a film where I played a wedding guest. I even booked an international commercial for *Tiger Beer*, as well as a commercial for a cookie company, playing a grandma.

I had a ball serving as the "Grand Dame" of the X (Extreme) Games for ESPN, where I had to be on a skateboard, wear tattoos and a dog collar. So at the young age 82, I began a new career as an actress.

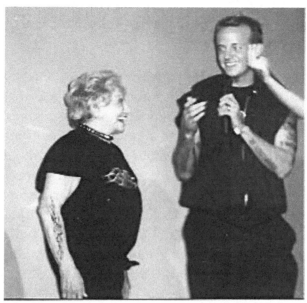

Here I am as the "Grand Dame" of the X Games for ESPN, with tattoos, dog collar, and skate board.

Chapter 13- Traveling the World in Style

When Lillian moved back to Los Angeles from NYC, she didn't want me to be alone. So she moved me into her home. Living with her was exciting. Every day, I seemed to experience new and different things. I sang in play, went to exercise classes, to spas, where I got messages and was pampered. I socialized with Lillian and her friends. For the first time, I was enjoying my life to the fullest.

"Let yourself be pampered and enjoy it to the fullest."

When Lillian was 10, she made me a Birthday card which read" *Mommy, one day I will take you around the world.*" What Lillian wrote on that card eventually came true. She took me around the world.

Some of the trips were for pleasure, while others were for Lillian's business. For the next 10 years, she and I became world travelers.

The countries which I visited were: *Antigua, Argentina, Aruba, Australia, Austria, Barbados Barbuda, Brazil, Bulgaria, Canada, Canary Islands, Cayman Islands, Chile, China, Costa Rica, Cyprus, Denmark, Dominican Republic, Dubai, England, Egypt, Estonia, Falkland Islands, Faroe Islands, Finland, France, Germany, Gibraltar, Greece, Greenland, Hong Kong, Iceland, India, Ireland, Israel, Italy, Jamaica, Japan, Kenya, Macau, Madagascar, Malaysia, Mauritius, Mexico, Monaco, Mongolia, Morocco, Netherlands, New Zealand, Norway, Oman, Panama, Peru, Poland, Puerto Rico, Qatar, Reunion, Romania, Russia, Spain, Saint Lucia, Saint Martin, Scotland, Seychelles, Shetland Islands, Singapore, Sweden, Switzerland, Taiwan, Thailand, Tunisia, Turkey, Ukraine, United Arab Emirates, United States (all 50 states) Uruguay, and the Virgin Islands.*

As you read the second part of my book, you will see photos of me at some of these exotic destinations.

Return to Poland

During my travels, after 8 decades, I was finally able to return to Poland. It was a rewarding experience for me for number of reasons.

First of all, I visited the hospital where I was born - "Baby Jesus Hospital." It was so exciting for me to return to a place where I literally began my life.

Next, I was able to pay my respects to my family, who perished in the Holocaust. Lillian dug a makeshift grave and we buried photographs of my father, mother, brother, and sisters on the property of the home where I lived as a child. Lillian and I lit a candle, recited prayers, and sang songs to respect and honor their memory.

It was a very emotional experience and something I had to do.

I also paid my respects at the various monuments honoring victims of the Holocaust and to those who fought for life up until the last minute. Seeing the monument commemorating those Poles who died in Siberia was also a very moving experience.

I was moved when I saw the monument in Warsaw, Poland, commemorating the Poles who were killed, murdered, and deported to labor camps in Siberia.

But perhaps the most emotional experience for me was to see one of my daughter's best- selling book, *Toxic People (Toksyczni Ludzie)* available in Polish bookstores and published in the same country I fled, due to Nazi oppression.

It was as though I survived the atrocities of the Nazis in Poland, and survived Siberia, so that my daughter could be born to touch millions of lives through her books. It chokes me up whenever I think about it.

My world famous daughter, Dr. Lillian Glass' book Toxic People in Polish

Return to Russia

My trip to Russia was equally fulfilling. As a former "Prisoner of War" during WWII, I was unwillingly taken to Siberia via cattle car under Joseph Stalin's regime. But this time, I was in Russia as a tourist, visiting Joseph Stalin's summer dacha in Sochi, Russia. It was surreal to be sipping wine and eating pastries in his living quarters, playing pool at his billiard table, and even more amazing that I lived to urinate in Stalin's personal toilet.

Most Treasured Experiences Abroad

Besides doing such extraordinary things like swimming in warm Lake Myvatn, Iceland when the weather was well below zero, seeing elephants, zebras, and monkey's up close in the Tsavo on a Kenyan safari, experiencing the Great Wall of China, seeing the pyramids in Egypt, visiting mosques in Morocco and Abu Dhabi, being sought out by a penguin in the Falkland Islands, and meeting extraordinary people like Aboriginals in Australia and Maoris in New Zealand, the most significant part of my travels was when I found myself face to face with Pope Benedict, who personally blessed me during his coronation.

Blessed By The Pope

My meeting with him clearly shows the power of one of my favorite sayings ***"positive thinking can create positive things."*** When I arrived in Italy with my daughter to visit the Vatican, we had no idea that it was the Coronation Day of the Pope Benedict, the German Pope. The streets were crowded and tours of Rome were limited. Lillian managed to secure a tour which stopped near the Vatican so we could see what was going on. The tour guide assured us that we would never get inside and said we would just have to observe what was going on from outside the gates.

"Before you trust others, trust yourself and your own instincts."

"Positive thinking creates positive things."

But I wasn't buying into the tour guide's negativity. I didn't trust what he said. Instead, I trusted my own instincts. I told my daughter" *I would like to see the pope.* ***Let's try. It may end up being in our favor."***

Lillian could not fathom how we could even try.
First of all, she wondered how would we would get into
the Vatican, past all the security guards. Secondly, the
place was enormous. It was like four football fields
away where the Pope was situated. But this didn't
deter me.

I just knew in my heart I would get to see the Pope. I
continued to trust my instincts.

All of a sudden, a security guard motioned to me to
come over to him as he opened a gate to allow me into
the premises.

As Lillian and I inched our way towards the massive
crowd, out of nowhere, an Italian woman grabbed my
hand and led me past one security gate to another,
until inch by inch, and step by step, Lillian
and I passed through all four massive security areas.

Miraculously, we found ourselves in the front, right
where all the cardinals and dignitaries were seated
and watching the proceedings. All of a sudden, Pope
Benedict stopped his Pope mobile directly in front of
me and personally blessed me, as you can see in the
photos of us which were taken at the exact moment he
blessed me.

As well you can see the expression on my face at that
exact moment I was blessed.

Pope Benedict personally blessing me during his Coronation at the Vatican.

The photo above shows my facial expression at the exact moment Pope Benedict was blessing me

Immediately after the coronation ceremony ended, cardinals, priests, and nuns from all over the world approached me, shook my hand, and gave me blessings as well. I am convinced that it was my positive thoughts in trying to get into the ceremony and trusting my instincts that created this positive experience.

Vatican-cardinals, priests, and nuns blessing me right after Pope Benedict's coronation

Embracing All Faiths

"If you respect your faith, you must respect another's faith."

I have a tremendous respect for people of all faiths. In fact, I have sought out centers for prayer and spirituality in the various countries I visited throughout the world. I prayed at a Hindu temple in Mumbai, India, a Buddhist temple in Singapore, and a Confucius Temple in Beijing, China. In the United States, I have attended and prayed at Mormon Church services as well as Christian, Jewish, Methodist, Episcopal, Protestant, and Greek Orthodox churches.

Left, at Wailing Wall in Jerusalem on the right in a Mosque in Abu Dhabi, UAE

In the photo to the left, I am saying prayers in both Hebrew and English as I placed a prayer note in the Wailing Wall in Jerusalem. In the photo to the right, I had just finished saying prayers in a mosque in Abu Dhabi. I also said prayers when I visited other mosques in Morocco, Dubai, Istanbul Turkey and Egypt. I strongly believe there would be more peace in the world if all people respected and better understood one another's religions. I believe that all religions have the same focus. They are all about love, treating each other well, and doing good in the world.

Chapter 14 - A Beauty Queen

Because of the war, I missed out on so many things teens and young women may experience. So, Lillian wanted me to experience something that she herself, experienced when she was a teenager - being a beauty queen. So, she entered me to compete in the Ms. Senior California Pageant.

"You're never too old to have sex appeal."

I picked out a sexy, low cut, form-fitting, hot pink, evening gown with rhinestone straps, which I wore for the occasion. For the talent portion of the competition, I sang "God Bless America" in my soprano voice.
It was one of the happiest days of my life and such a delightful surprise, to have been selected as "Miss Congeniality" in the Ms. Senior California Pageant at the age of 94. I cherish this honor to his day.

" Miss Congeniality" being kissed by a pageant official and a former Ms. Senior California.

Chapter 15- A Real Actress

When I moved back to Los Angeles fulltime, to be with my daughter, I became more serious about acting. So I enrolled in several acting classes and workshops.

I was lucky to get a commercial agent, who believed in me and sent me on auditions. I was able to book numerous commercials and television projects. Among them were *Western Film Festival, Google Glass, Hallmark Cards, Axe Deodorant,* a *Porsche,* and a *Blue Cross* commercial, where I played a senior bride.

Shooting a commercial for Hallmark Cards.

I also appeared in a reality show called *"Rolls Royce for a Day"* where I had to ride around in a Rolls Royce all day and do whatever I wanted to do, like partying and getting a big blue tattoo of a rose on my leg. Even though it was a fake one, it looked very real.

.

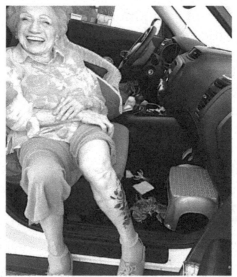

I am on the set of Rolls Royce for a Day with my realistic "fake" tattoo on my leg.

"Hesitate... You lose!"

"Since life is full of twists and turns, you must be flexible, so you can twist and turn thru life's ups and downs."

"Pity or worry never solves a problem. The only thing that does is ACTION. So take action!"

My most exciting commercial was doing the *"Dodge Wisdom"* commercial, "where I was able to say my favorite quote - one I lived by my entire life **Hesitate... you lose!** " I believe in never procrastinating and immediately seizing all opportunities which come my way.

At 19, I didn't hesitate for a moment after that Nazi soldier slapped me. I left Warsaw immediately, which was why I was able to survive. Throughout my life, I have taken action and full advantage of every opportunity that came my way.

I have always been flexible and kept an open mind. This allowed me to be ready and available for any new adventure that came my way.

Chapter 16- A New Career At 100 – Author, Counselor and Online Advice Giver

"You can do new things at any age. It's never too late!"

Writing this book has been extremely rewarding for me because it has allowed me to share with people from all over the world and from every walk of life, the most important and valuable things I've learned over these past ten decades.

I love the fact that with modern technology, people can now store my book on their mobile devices through ebook and always have it available to them. I am even more thrilled that they can even hear my sayings, spoken in my own voice when they listen to my downloaded audiotape of this book. I could never have imagined something like this was possible 100 years ago.

Had the war not broken out, I would have gone to college to become a psychiatrist or psychologist. I could have afforded to pay for all of my education with the money I earned as a shirt manufacturer and seller. What that was not meant to be at that time. What is meant to be at this time is that I am making myself available to everyone over the internet to give you my personal advice on any personal question, problem, or issue which you may have in your life.

While I won't be performing psychotherapy, where a license is required, I am offering you my personal opinions and my advice, based on all my knowledge and my 100 years of experience.

Perhaps I can help you and your loved ones see things more clearly and help solve your problem from my perspective. Whether it's a relationship problem, career or work related issue, or any personal concern, I am here to answer any of your personal questions anywhere the world.

All you have to do is go to my website at www.rosaleeglass.com to find out how to send me your specific and personal questions and concerns, so that I can provide you with my feedback.

"Until you start something, everything seems difficult."

At 100 years of age, I am excited to embark on a new career as an online counselor and advice giver. While everything is difficult before you start doing it, once I get started I have the confidence my new business will be successful in reaching those who may need my help and guidance.

Chapter 17- Dogsledding and the Northern Lights to Celebrate 100 Years

"Never look backward. Only look forward."

"Never be afraid to try new things that make you feel uncomfortable. You may end up liking it."

In celebration of my 100 years on this earth, I am embarking on a new and exciting adventure of my lifetime.

I am bundling up, dressing as warm as possible and going to Alaska to will do something I always wanted to do - see the green Northern Lights and go on a ride pulled by Iditarod sled dogs.

I plan to live each day of the rest of my life with joy and excitement as I try new and different things and meet more wonderful people.

My message to you is that it is never too late to try and do something new or to do something you have always wanted to do- even if you are a century old.

PART II

Message About My Quotes

In the next section of this book, I would like to share with you some of my original quotes by which I have lived during my 10 decades of life. These quotes reflect my original personal philosophies of life. They have motivated me throughout my life and are what keep me going, as I continue to maintain both a realistic and a positive outlook on life.

Hopefully, my quotes will motivate you, just like they have motivated and inspired others, especially my daughter, Lillian. She has always told me that she attributes a large part of her success in her life to these motivating words, I will now be sharing with you.

It is my intention to inspire and motive you through these "words of wisdom." Perhaps they will allow you to see life a little differently. Perhaps they will give you a different perspective on life.

Perhaps they can make a more positive difference for you as you go through all of its' ups and downs and twists and turns.

Rosalee Glass Original
Words of Wisdom

My gift to you – my original words of Wisdom

HESITATE....
YOU LOSE!

Appearing in the "Dodge Wisdom" Commercial shown during the 2105 Super Bowl, saying "Hesitate... You lose!"

NEVER GIVE UP!

No Matter how
difficult it

seems,

just try again until
you make it.

Me on the set for a GOOGLE Glasses commercial which I did.

TALK TO THE HEAD...

NOT TO THE TAIL

If you want to get something accomplished don't go through subordinates who have no power to do anything for you. Instead talk to the head or the boss if you want to accomplish something and get results.

BEING AROUND
SMALL MINDED
PEOPLE KEEPS YOU
SMALL

BEING AROUND **BIG**
MINDED PEOPLE
KEEPS
YOU **BIG**

A mutual admiration between me and Magic Johnson at Laker Vice President Bill Sharman's honor celebration.

NEVER LOOK BACKWARD

ONLY LOOK FORWARD

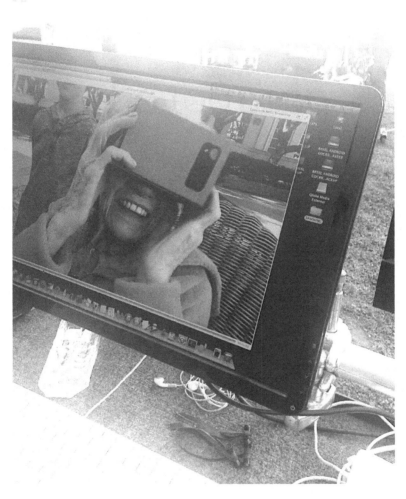

Here I am in a monitor looking through GOOGLE glasses for a GOOGLE Glass commercial I did.

Let yourself be
pampered

and enjoy it to the
fullest.

Me being pampered having makeup done on the set for my GOOGLE GLASS commercial.

Positive Thinking Can Create Positive Things

Pope Benedict at his Coronation looking directly at me while he is blessing me.

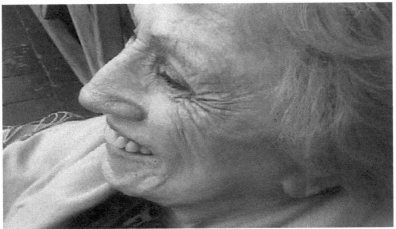

Me looking directly at Pope Benedict at the exact moment he s blessing me at his Coronation Ceremony at the Vatican.

ALWAYS TRY!

It may turn out in your favor!

Me appearing on a video monitor at an audition for a Merrill Lynch commercial.

Shoes Must Always Fit
Well.

Unless Your Feet Are
Happy...You Can't Be
Happy

Poor -fitting shoes can make you miserable. I suggest that if you wear heels, get them in a half a size larger in case your feet swell.

Be Thankful for What
You Have
And
Be Even More Thankful
For What You Don't
Have

The Glass Girls- Me Lillian and Annabella truly grateful that we have each other's backs.

Your Character

Means Everything -

It Is Really All

That You Have

Here I am on one of the many cruise ships I went on to see the world.

You MUST Exercise and Move your Body

Me doing my Pilates exercises on my AeroPilates reformer, which I love.

You can never send a cat to get you a bottle of milk, because they will usually drink it themselves.

Likewise, you can never send a competitive or jealous person get you something because they will usually take it themselves.

NEVER GO TO A PARTY WHERE YOU ARE NOT TRULY WELCOME!

Only go to places where you are wanted and welcome with open arms.

Even in the coldest and saddest days,

the SUN can still come out to

SHINE for YOU

Al

l bundled up on a chilly Los Angeles day, but enjoying the warm sun as I read a
magazine in a Beverly Hills Park.

A LIAR CAN BE A THIEF!

IF SOMEONE CAN LIE

TO YOU

THEY CAN ALSO STEAL FROM YOU

Stay away from anyone who is *jealous* of YOU

or tries to *compete* with YOU because

they will only try to *destroy* YOU

Dressed in wrestling gear for a book photo shoot about seniors doing athletics.

Always listen to your

STOMACH

When it's EMPTY it will tell

you when to

START eating

When it's FULL it will tell

you when to STOP eating

Eating a nutritious breakfast of Greek yogurt with fresh blueberries.

When you are
well~dressed and

well ~groomed,

people will treat you with

more respect

Dressed elegantly for a Porsche commercial..

SPEAK OUT!

Open your mouth.
Never hold things in
if something bothers
you.

Ready to speak out.

INNER BEAUTY

SHOWS ON A

PERSON'S FACE

My daughter Dr. Lillian Glass headed out to do a television interview.

ONLY WHEN YOU HAVE ENOUGH INFORMATION CAN YOU MAKE THE RIGHT DECISION

Annabella Glass deciding which of her favorite toys she will choose.

NO ONE ASKS "HOW ARE YOU 5 YEARS AGO?"

INSTEAD THEY ASK "HOW ARE YOU?" (meaning) NOW

...IT IS ONLY NOW THAT REALLY COUNTS

At a photo shoot in Los Angeles, California. The only thing that matters is NOW!

YOU'LL NEVER

BE IN FINANCIAL
TROUBLE

IF YOU SPEND ONLY
WHAT YOU CAN
AFFORD

AND SAVE UP FOR
WHAT YOU WANT

Standing near the Rolls Royce I rode in for a reality show I did called "Rolls Royce for a Day."

You can learn
something from
anyone-
including
animals

A lone penguin in the Falkland Islands left his other penguin friends behind to run up to greet me. Perhaps he thought he and I were long lost relatives as we seem to be dressed alike. Observe the penguin's body language. Its' feet are pointed directly at my feet. This means that he really liked me and vice versa.

Two Shetland ponies in the Faroe Islands approached me and kissed my hands.

Visiting some recently shaved alpacas in the Chilean countryside.

Two loves of my life. Above is Annabella my golden doodle (whom I named) and below is my lhasa apso, Lambear, who lived to be 120 in doggie years.

WHEN YOU'RE INDEPENDENT, YOU CAN PLAY YOUR OWN DRUM ANY WAY

YOU LIKE

Playing a drum in the island of Mauritius in the Indian Ocean.

Fun-loving and upbeat

friends

are life's

Precious Gifts.

Me with two of my dear friends, Playboy Playmates, Elke Jeinsen and Barbara Moore.

Colors reflect life~

If you want to feel happy,

surround yourself with bright colors.

Wearing colorful attire, ready to go into a commercial audition.

Learn from all cultures. While we may look and act different, deep down we are really all alike.

In New Zealand, visiting native Maoris after watching them perform a Haka.

IF YOU RESPECT YOUR FAITH YOU MUST RESPECT ANOTHER'S FAITH

At a mosque in Abu Dhabi in the United Arab Emirates.

YOU CAN DO NEW THINGS AT ANY AGE. IT'S NEVER TOO LATE.

Trying something new- going up in a hot air balloon.

IF YOU WANT TO BE TRULY HAPPY

NEVER LIVE IN THE PAST

Dressed in bicycle attire riding my stationary bicycle. It's part of my daily exercise program which I do at home.

EVEN IF YOU DON'T
FEEL LIKE IT,
SMILE ANYWAY.
YOU WILL
IMMEDIATELY START
TO FEEL BETTER AND
HAPPIER.

Me smiling.

Eating Bread and drinking water with someone you love, is better than eating a gourmet meal with someone whom can't stand.

Me and the "apple of my eye" – my loving daughter Lillian, together in Punta Arenas, Argentina.

Until You Start Something Everything Seems Difficult

Me wearing a silk nightgown and getting ready to start my day.

Never be afraid
to try new
things that
make you feel
uncomfortable.
You may end up
liking it.

Me in the swimming pool with my water therapy instructor Kevin Wagner. At first I was hesitant in the pool, but then learned to love it.

If someone starts it with you,

FIGHT BACK!

DON'T LET ANYONE EVER

BEAT YOU UP

I am wearing a wrestling outfit for a photo shoot for a book on senior athletes.

ALWAYS LISTEN TO YOUR HEART AND YOUR INSTINCTS!

ACT UPON THEM!

IF THEY TELL YOU SOMETHING IS WRONG – IT IS!

Looking at and listening to the crashing waves in Honolulu, Hawaii.

Since life is full of Twists and
Turns,

You must be Flexible so that
you can

Twist and Turn through life's
Ups and Downs

I am sitting on an elegant swing in Mumbai, India.

If something goes
wrong,

immediately think of
what to do next!

On a train ride in New Zealand, thinking what I will do next.

Listen carefully to EVERYTHING someone says about themselves.

If they tell you they are a bad person, they probably they are.

After all, they know more about who they are than anyone else.

Here I am carefully listening to someone telling me all about themselves.

Neither PITY nor WORRY ever solves a problem.

The only thing that solves it is ACTION.

SO TAKE ACTION

I always believe that you must take immediate action in all that you want to do.

One who BRINGS
gossip to you-

will often

CARRY gossip
about you.

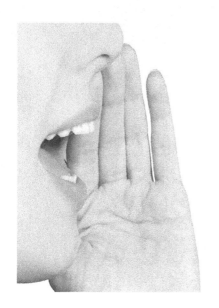

BEFORE YOU TRUST OTHERS,
TRUST YOURSELF AND YOUR OWN INSTINCTS

I always trust my instincts and it never fails..

ALWAYS THINK

BEFORE YOU ACT

I am in Copenhagen, Denmark in front of the Little Mermaid.

Speak up!

But when you do, make sure it makes sense

Speaking in front of the audience and judges at the Ms. Senior California Pageant where she won the title of "Miss Congeniality."

Don't go on and on when
you tell a story.

Instead, make sure that
your story has a

beginning, middle, and an
end.

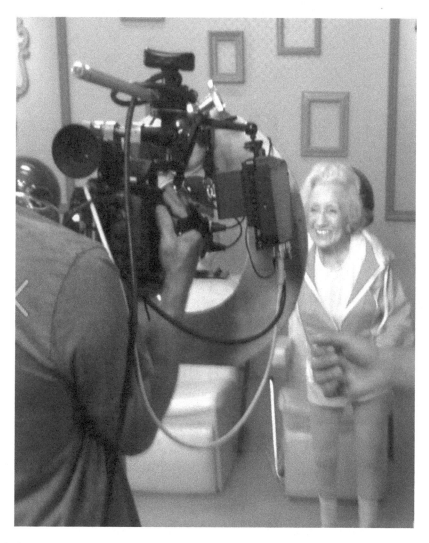

Doing a commercial shoot in front of the camera for Hallmark Cards.

Luck is doing the right thing and taking a chance.

Dressed as a bride for a Blue Cross commercial campaign.

Never allow

anyone to

belittle you.

In a *wrestling outfit and ready to wrestle for a photo shoot on a book of seniors and sports.*

TO SURVIVE

DIFFICULT TIMES

DON'T FALL APART -

BE STRONG

THINK POSITIVE

Lifting what looks like a 200 lb. weight, but it was really made of a lightweight plastic. I am on the set of a photo shoot for a book on sports.

DON'T BE OLD FASHIONED-

GO WITH THE TIMES

In my " gangsta" pose.

Don't be jealous or compare yourself with anyone. You are uniquely <u>You</u> and they are uniquely <u>Them</u>.

Me with dear friend Joyce Sharman and my daughter Lillian Glass at Joyce's charity event honoring her husband, the great basketball legend Bill Sharman.

Nothing can make you feel better than a good belly laugh

Enjoying a hearty laugh.

If you stand up straight & hold your head high, you'll always look better in clothes

In front of the Roxbury Center in Beverly Hills, standing with straight posture and head held high.

See Your Doctor Regularly.

Most illness

can be treated successfully if they are caught early.

Me with my favorite doctor and star of "Biggest Loser" - Dr. Robert Huizenga giving me a thumbs up!

Know where your purse, wallet, and cell phone are at all times.

Me with my purse close by my side .

Never put yourself down

On the set of a Porsche commercial I did.

When you work hard for your money, you will appreciate it more than if the money is given to you.

Earning my own money means a lot to me. Here I am earning some money for filming the "Dodge Wisdom" commercial which was shown during the 2015 Super Bowl.

Always have money put away which you never touch and only use when you REALLY need it.

A good nap and a good bowel movement can clear your mind, stop crankiness, and even allow you to function better.

Here I am feeling chipper and ready to take on the rest of the day after taking an afternoon nap.

If something isn't working for

you, stop and take a break.

Then calmly and intelligently try

to figure out how you can make it

work.

I'm taking a break at the beautiful Self Realization Center in Pacific Palisades, California.

Treat loved ones you
love the very best.
Never treat
strangers better
than the way
you treat the people
you love.

Portrait of the three "Glass Girls"- me, Annabella, and Lillian Glass.

Don't become greedy when it comes to food.

Eat or drink what you need so you that you won't end up

throwing it out or throwing it up.

Dressed in green and having one of my favorite green health food drinks in Bel Air, California.

Pay close attention to how someone looks at you when greeting you.

A dirty mean look with no smile, tells how negatively they really feel about you.

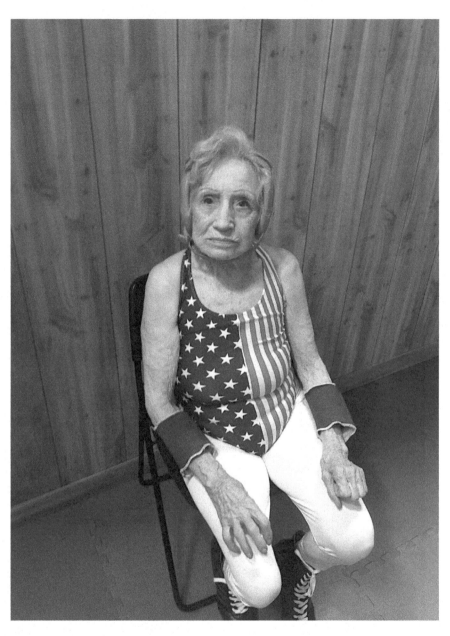

In my wrestling gear and looking fierce for my photo shoot.

When you have

Love in your

Heart, Others

Can Easily

Love You

I love getting hugged and kissed by all of these handsome men around the world.

Surround
yourself with
those who
make you smile
and laugh.

Here I am with some new friends I made at a Swedish Viking celebration in Stockholm, Sweden

If you respect
yourself,

others will quickly
realize that they
too,

must treat you with
respect.

Here I am on set with my co-star of AXE Deodorant commercial.

You are never too old

to have

SEX APPEAL

I am dressed in a sexy hot pink evening gown at the Ms. Senior California Pageant where I won "Miss Congeniality

Do something for
someone
with no expectation
that you may get
something in return.

Here I am doing something nice for Annabella- giving her a welcomed body massage and not expecting anything from her in return..

Surround yourself

with colors and

objects

that are

"candy to your eyes."

As usual, I am , colorfully dressed, sitting on my colorful couch, at home.

A few minutes until night is still not night.

Anything can

still happen in your favor up until the last minute.

Only when you pay careful attention to what's going on around you,

will you see the message

the universe is giving you

about what direction to take in life.

Me and my golden doodle dog Annabella on "Rosalee Road" which is a private road that was made just for me in Bel Air, California.

Never think you are
above anyone else.
Treat everyone like
you would a
King or a Queen.

Beauty Queen contestant and winner, "Miss Congeniality.".

Life is like having a meal.

Sometimes you'll enjoy it and other times you won't.

Here I am at a restaurant in Buenos Aires, Argentina. I got a free meal just because the owner liked my smile.

Don't wait for others to make you happy or to make things happen for YOU.
It's up to YOU to do that!

Here I am very happily taking a stroll in the park in Beverly Hills, California.

Seeing the world opens your heart, mind, and soul.

I am standing outside a cafe in Malta.

As a naturalized American citizen, I was proud to visit Mt. Rushmore.

I loved seeing all the animals on a Safari in Kenya, Africa

I loved swimming in the warm lake, while it was cold at Lake Myvatn in Iceland

Posing with a camel statue in Abu Dhabi in the United Arab Emirates.

Here I am in amazing Dubai in front of the Burj Al Arab overlooking the water.

MANY HAPPY MOMENTS

ARE WHAT MAKES

A HAPPY PERSON

A very happy moment for me was when I went onstage and sang together with famed Argentinian singer, Daniel Bouchet.

Another happy moment was with my daughter Lillian in Stockholm, Sweden sitting on a bench which was made of ice.

Never speak sweetly to someone's face and bitterly behind their back.

Doing a short film in the South Bay in Los Angeles, where I played a grandmother, hugging the star of the show who is eating a burrito.

Not everyone will like You

And

you won't like everyone

Here I am in my wrestling gear for a book photo shoot on seniors doing sports.

Time goes by anyway, so you might as well do something worth-while each day.

Here I am with a bamboo stalk I planted. I am bringing it to a friend as a housewarming gift.

Always be grateful
and humble when
good things
happen for you.
Never let it go to
your head.

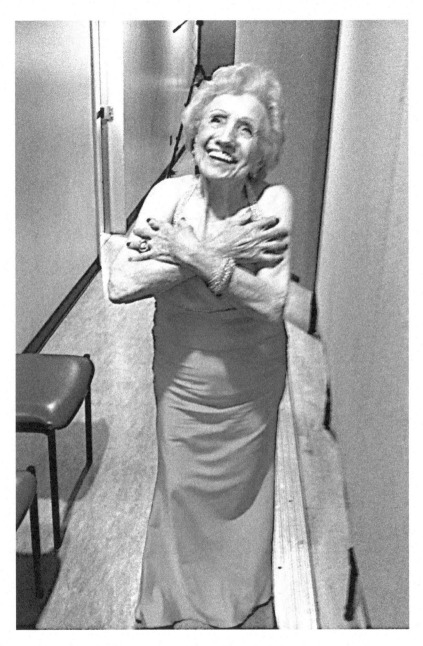

Truly grateful I won "Miss Congeniality" at the Ms. Senior California Pageant.

For a
heartfelt hug,
press your
heart
against theirs.

I am giving a heart to heartfelt hug to one of my favorite people, my friend Paul Sweeney in Westwood, California.

WHEN YOU JUST DON'T LIKE SOMEONE, YOUR INSTINCTS ARE WARNING YOU TO "BE CAREFUL" AND "STAY AWAY"

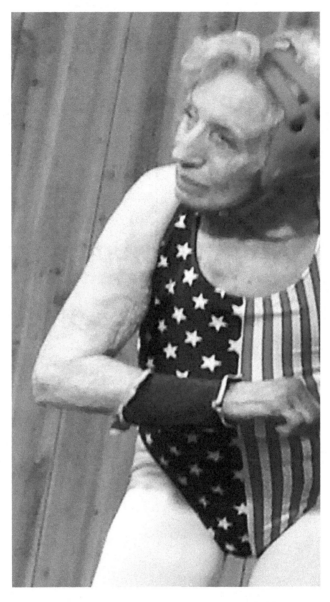

Wearing my wrestling gear modeling for a book on seniors doing sports.

It doesn't matter what you sing or how you sound when you sing.

Just sing from your heart because singing is healing.

I'm at a Fourth of July Celebration at the Rose Bowl in Pasadena California loudly and proudly singing the national anthem. The couple across from me to my left are listening to me sing. Afterwards, they said they loved my singing voice.

Be loyal
and fight
for those you
believe in and
love.

Here I am with my boxing gloves on, delivering a punch for a photo shoot.

ALWAYS MAKE SURE YOU ARE DRESSED WARM ENOUGH

I am warmly bundled up at the Great Wall of China.

Losing someone you love is the worst pain possible. Knowing that you treated them well throughout their life and gave them lots of love helps ease that pain.

I was very somber in Warsaw, Poland paying respects to my family who were among the 6 million Jews killed by the Nazi's.

Me and Lillian in front of the Warsaw Ghetto Uprising Monument in Warsaw.

231

Only after
you've
experienced
bitter times

can you
appreciate the
sweet times

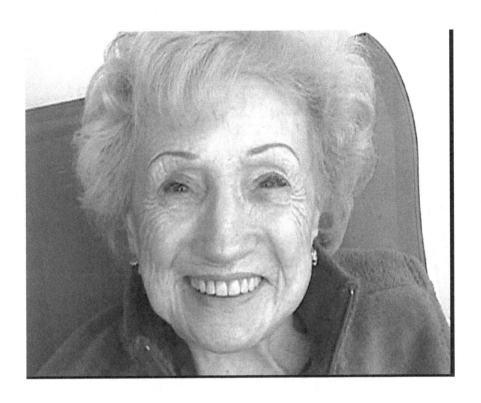

After the hell I once lived, I appreciate everything in my life.

LIFE is your
most precious
possession.
You MUST
always FIGHT
for it!

I am wearing my boxing gloves and ready for my boxing lesson.

If you are feeling stressed, nervous, anxious, or upset,

immediately drop your shoulders

take in a deep breath and then exhale slowly.

It will calm you down so you can relax and think more clearly.

Even though I am concerned about what's wrong with my computer, you would never know it from this photo. I dropped my shoulders, took a deep breath, and relaxed so I could better deal with everything.

Listen to everyone's opinions, but think for yourself

While I always value my daughter Lillian's opinions, in the final analysis, I always make up my own mind and following my own thoughts.

Bad times are

not forever

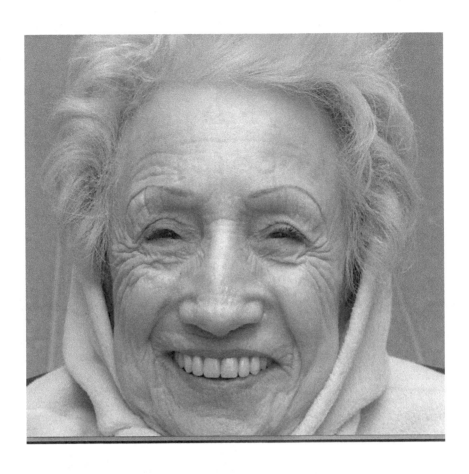

Whenever feel disappointed, I always remind myself that bad times are not forever.

A NEGATIVE EXPERIENCE

CAN OFTEN
LEAD YOU
TO THE

RIGHT ROAD.

I am definitely on the right road – "Rosalee Road.."

If you really
believe
you can
do something,
don't ever let
anyone tell you
that you can't do it.

Here I am dressed in a cream colored outfit posing for a photo shoot as I sit on a matching cream colored trunk.

If you ever feel shy
around someone,

just keep asking
them questions

like a journalist
would do

My daughter Lillian got rid of her shyness when she was young, after I told her to act like a journalist and ask people questions. Now she is a real journalist, among the other things she does professionally.

Treat everyone with the same respect no matter who they are

Here I am with legendary screen icon, Jane Russell who was a guest at one of my parties.

Cherish those who show you love and kindness

Famed Argentinian singer Damiel Bouchet serenading me at one of his performances in Orlando, Floridia

WRONG
THINGS
DON'T TURN
OUT RIGHT

As an online Advice Giver, I am reading an email from someone who wrote me about something they did wrong in their relationship.

Always Act

Classy

Here I am on a classy photo shoot for the cover of this book.

Conclusion

While life doesn't always go smoothly, life is truly a blessing. In these 100 years I have spent on this earth, I can attest to the fact that one's happiness depends on how one looks at the things which happen to them in life.

I would have been bitter after receiving a slap over my face for no reason from the Nazi soldier when I was 19.

I could have become even more bitter after witnessing firsthand the enormous cruelty and inhumanity of what Nazi's did to innocent people from throwing babies out of windows to brutally beating and killing people before my eyes.

I could have easily become bitter when I lost my parents Mendel and Perla and my two sisters Regina and Lola in my 20's, due to the horrors of the Holocaust and did not have the luxury of having them with me throughout my adult life.

I could have become bitter after I lost my brother, Jacob after he was unwillingly taken from a train and forced into the Russian army, where no one ever knew what happened to him.

I could have become bitter after losing my two precious babies due to the horrific conditions of war and not being able to give them food, proper nutrition, warmth, shelter, and medical attention.

I could have become bitter for the physical and emotional abuse I endured while being a victim of forced slave labor in a bitter cold Siberian Prison camp in Russia.

I could have become bitter that life was such a financial struggle when I worked long hours with little money in order to feed my family when I came to America.

I could have become biter that I did not get financial reparations from Germany for the upheaval they caused in my life, simply because of the technicality that I was in a Siberian Prison camp in Russia as opposed to a Concentration camp in Poland or Germany.

I could have become bitter because my husband suffered health problems and I had to be the bread-winner of the family in order to put food on the table.

I could have become bitter because I had so little money that I could not afford to buy a dress, go out to a restaurant for dinner, or even see a movie.

I could have become bitter after my beloved husband of 60 years died, leaving me feeling lost and empty.

I could have become bitter after my precious, loving, intelligent, and charismatic son Manny, was killed so unnecessarily at the hands of and incompetent doctors in New Jersey.

I could have become bitter at the insensitive, cold, non-compassionate doctor who was only a doctor for 7 months and who improperly intubated my son, rendering him a vegetable until he died.

But I chose not to allow bitterness or hate to consume me. Instead, I picked myself up and as reflected through these words of wisdom that I have shared with you.

I have been able to overcome some of the most miserable times in life that anyone can imagine. I have remained positive, loving, kind, sincere, and compassionate. I do not harbor hate. Instead, I only harbor love in my heart.

Having experienced a "living hell" in the first half of my life, I am truly grateful and I so appreciative for the "heaven on earth" which I have lived. The bad times did not last forever. That should be a lesson for you as well. Know that your bad times will not last forever.

The second half of my life, even though it has had its moments of pain and anguish, with the loss of my husband, and my Manny, I am grateful for all that I do have. While my family is small with only my daughter Lillian and my dog Annabella, with no other blood relatives, I feel that Lillian is worth 10 children, as an Indian man once remarked to me about her.

She is the catalyst who has motivated me and helped allow me to live out my dreams, explore my talents, and embark upon new horizons. I certainly could not have done it without her. She has been my "stage mother" and manager in my acting career, which I began at the age of 82. As a result, I have been blessed to have appeared in films, television shows, and in numerous commercials. As the tables have turned, she has also acted as a nurturing and protective "mother" towards me.

She helped give me back the teen hood, and young adulthood that I never had due to life's circumstances and the terror of war. She provided me with the opportunity to attend dancing lessons, acting classes, tai chi classes, exercise classes, piano lesson and introduced me to Pilates. She has taken me to glamorous Black Tie affairs and show business functions, where she introduced me to many celebrities.

She allowed me to live up to my potential as I experienced a whole new dimension of life. She allowed me to experience the things I missed earlier in my life. She even entered me into a beauty pageant for seniors Like any proud "stage mother," she cried tears of joy for me when I won "Miss Congeniality."

She opened my world by taking me with her when she gave lectures around the country and around the world. I was able to see places I never even dreamed about because of her. I will never forget when she was 10 years old and made me a Birthday card with a picture of a globe that she drew. Inside the card she wrote, *"Dear Mommy, I will give you this Birthday present when I get older. I will take you around the globe. Love, Lily"* True to her word, and many decades later, Lily made good on her promise to me as she took me all over the globe and provided me with such exciting experiences I could never imagine.

I have been up in a hot air balloon, gone to such exotic places as Mauritius and Madagascar. I have seen the ancient pyramids and sphinx in Egypt, swam in warm Lake Myvatn, Iceland while it was freezing cold outside. I Rode in a jeep on a safari in Kenya where I saw zebras, elephants, and monkey's up close. I went to the Great Wall of China. I learned the Maori greeting of pressing my nose and forehead against another person's, while they did the same as we both breathed in one another. I watched the Maori's do a Haka dance in New Zealand and met an aboriginal man in Australia who allowed me to play his precious musical instrument. I ate the finest exotic foods during my travels and spent an exciting cold winter, dressed warmly, in all the Scandinavian countries where I experienced the Christmas markets. I relished in the Greek Islands as I soaked in the sun and azure blue Aegean Sea. I was thrilled to walk on the same ground as the Olympians of ancient Greece did in Olympia. I went to beautiful mosques in Egypt, Abu Dhabi, Oman, Dubai, and shopped at the world famous ancient Grand Bazaar in Turkey for leather jackets of all colors. Lillian usually wears these jackets on her many television appearances. I floated in the Dead Sea and prayed at the Wailing Wall in Jerusalem.

At the Vatican, I inched my way across four large football like fields through countless security crossings, step by step, until I was able to stand directly in front of the German Pope Benedict at his coronation, where he looked directly at me and personally blessed me. What a gift to be personally blessed by a German Pope. His blessing helped heal my emotional pain as a result of all the atrocities that I experienced as a result of the Germans in WWII.

What another gift it was for me to meet priests and cardinals from Ireland, Africa, India, Germany and Italy who each blessed me on their way out of the Coronation ceremonies. It is an experience I cherish regularly as my heart fills with joy whenever I look at their photos on my wall.

It was also a healing for me to return to Warsaw, Poland after over eight decades and visit the hospital where I was born (Baby Jesus Hospital) and run up and down the steps with excitement. I found the street and the location of the home where I grew up in Warsaw. There, Lillian and I paid our respects to my parents, brother and sisters by digging up the ground, making a makeshift grave, where we lovingly placed each of their photographs and covered it with flowers, lit a candle, and sang prayers of mourning as tears rolled down our cheeks. What made me the proudest was seeing my daughter's book published by Rebis Publishing in a Polish bookstore- "*Toxic People*". It was surreal to think that my entire family perished and that I survived so my beautiful and brilliant daughter could be born to write a best-selling book "*Toxic People*" which would touch and heal so many people's lives around the world

Perhaps the most surreal experience was to be back in Russia. Only this time, it was not in a harsh Siberian prison camp. Instead it was at the luxurious Russian, Sochi dacha of the man who was ultimately responsible for my being a Prisoner of War and for my brother Jacob's death – the brutal dictator Joseph Stalin. In his dacha, I ate pastry, drank wine, played pool with his billiard sticks and most poetic of all, I was thrilled to have the opportunity to urinate in his personal toilet as Lillian and I both laughed hysterically.

After I did the *Dodge Wisdom* Super Bowl commercial, people kept asking me if I had other words of wisdom for them. I did. That is why, with Lillian's encouragement, I decided to share all of my words of wisdom with you through this book. These words have not only helped Lillian throughout her life, by they helped me through my own life's ups and downs. It is my wish that they do the same for you.

Now in my 100th year, my example and my message to you to you is that it is never too late to live out your dreams.

I have always wanted to be a therapist and a counselor. If circumstances would have been different, I would have gone to medical school or to graduate school when I was in my 20's and I would have become a psychiatrist or psychologist. There is no question about it.

I could have easily afforded to pay for my education to become a psychiatrist or psychologist with the money I earned as a successful young business woman, manufacturing men's dress shirts and selling them to stores around Warsaw.

While I won't be treating anyone's mental health disorder or doing actual psychotherapy, I am available via the internet to give anyone, no matter where they live or what language the speak (with the help of Google translate), my personal opinion concerning any problem that might bother them.

Whether it is a dating, marriage, or relationship problem, a career, or work related issue, a family concern, or any personal issue, I am here to help you.

Perhaps my 100 years of experience can be of value to you in giving you yet another set of eyes to look at give particular problem and to then give you my personal perspective.

For the rest of the time I have left on this earth, I plan to take full advantage of this gift of life.

I will continue to do things I have always wanted to do, like go dogsledding and see the Northern lights on my actual birthday of January 28th.

I want to continue to experience new and exciting adventures in new and exciting places and meet more and more wonderful people.

And most of all, I want to continue on with my positive attitude and outlook on life. I want to continue to give and receive love. That is the absolute secret to making it to 100.

May God Bless you always.

Rosalee Glass

About the Author

Rosalee Glass was born in 1917 in Warsaw Poland at Baby Jesus Hospital. Developing a knack for sewing, at age 15, she made men's shirts which she sold to a neighborhood haberdashery. At age 18 she had a successful business with 10 employees and sold her shirts to numerous stores in the Warsaw area. Also at 18 she met the love of her life, Abraham Glass, a violin player, who serenaded her outside her home and whom she married at 19 and remained with him for the next 60 years until he died at the age of 90.

All was well, until the couple took a stroll and for no reason at all, a Nazi soldier slapped Rosalee across the face. She knew it was time to leave Warsaw. So she and Abraham miraculously crossed the border from where the German's had occupied to Russian territory in northern Poland for safety.

But it wasn't safe there either, as Russian soldiers kidnapped them, threw them into cattle cars, and made them do forced labor in the brutally freezing Siberian forest where they lacked food, clothing and shelter. From Siberia, they were kidnapped and taken to Kazakhstan, where they lived in a chicken coup. Due to the hellish conditions in both Siberia and Kazakhstan, tragically, Rosalee lost two children

Rosalee, her husband and surviving young son were rounded up and taken to a displaced person's camp in Germany, and were subsequently granted entry into the United States.

Grateful to be in a free country, Rosalee added a baby girl, Lily, to her small family as they struggled culturally and economically. Rosalee called upon her excellent sewing skills and started a drapery manufacturing business which allowed her to support her family for close to three decades. After retiring, she and Abraham moved to California, settling into a comfortable retirement community until Abraham's death at age 90. Three years later, tragedy struck as Rosalee's son Manny, was wrongly intubated by a novice doctor and became a vegetable and died, devastating Rosalee. It made her want to take life by the reins and live everyday her life to the fullest

She decided to live out all her dreams and do things she never did before – travel the world, take tai chi, dance, and acting lessons. This led to her to becoming an actress at age 82. She appeared in plays, films, and a reality show. Some of her commercials include *Tiger Beer, Western Film Festival, AXE Deodorant, Porsche, Hallmark Cards, and Blue Cross* (where she played a senior bride). She became the *Grande Dame"* of the X *Games* for ESPN, and was featured in a reality show *"Rolls Royce for a Day."*

At age 90, she walked on the Great Wall of China and went on a Safari in Africa and traveled the rest of the world. At age 94, she won "Miss Congeniality" in the Ms. Senior California Pageant. At 97, millions saw her award winning *"Dodge Wisdom"* commercial appearance where she was featured saying *"Hesitate...you lose"* - a saying she lived by all of her life.

At 99 she not only took up Pilates, she wrote this book documenting other original sayings to inspire and help guide people through the ups and downs of their life.

At 100 she is embarking on a new career as counselor and advice giver whereby people can email for her personal advice on relationship, family, personal, or work related issues. She also plans to embrace life by meeting more wonderful people and going on adventures like going dogsledding and seeing the Northern lights.

Rosalee lives in Los Angeles with her beloved daughter, Dr. Lillian Glass and adorable golden doddle, Annabella. For more information about her products go to www.rosaleeglass.com

Additional Products

Additional products related to this book. They include:

1. Audiotapes of Rosalee Glass actually reading her original Words of Wisdom.
    You can purchase the tape at www.rosaleeglass.com or on www.amazon.com

2. Framed Wall Hangings of Rosalee Glass' Original Words of Wisdom www.rosaleeglass.com

3. Consulting services with Rosalee Glass. After 100 years, she has seen it and heard it all. She is available to provide you with her personal advice on any problem you may have.

Sometimes getting sage advice from a centurion may be all that you need.
Email her at rosaleeglass@hotmail.com or call 310-274-0528

4. For Books, ebooks, audiotapes and videotapes by Rosalee Glass' daughter Dr. Lillian Glass go to www.drlillianglass.com or amazon.com

Dr. Lillian Glass' books and tapes include:

Talk to Win
World of Words
Say It Right
Confident Conversation
He Says She Says
Toxic People
Attracting Terrific People
Complete Idiot's Guide to Understanding Men and Women
Complete Idiot's Guide to Verbal Self Defense
I Know What You're Thinking Toxic Men
Body Language of Terrorists
The Body Language Advantage
The Body Language of Liars
50 Ways My Dog Made Me Into A Better Person
Bikram Vocal Yoga

Made in USA - Kendallville, IN
1217951_9781929873562
12.28.2020 1253